Margaritas

Margaritas

MORE THAN 45 CLASSIC & CONTEMPORARY RECIPES

**DAVID T. SMITH
& KELI RIVERS**

photography by
Alex Luck

RYLAND PETERS & SMALL
LONDON • NEW YORK

Senior designer Toni Kay
Production manager
  Gordana Simakovic
Editorial director Julia Charles
Creative director Leslie Harrington
Food stylist Lorna Brash
Prop stylist Luis Peral

Indexer Hilary Bird

First published in 2024 by
Ryland Peters & Small
20–21 Jockey's Fields
London WC1R 4BW
and
341 E 116th Street
New York, 10029

www.rylandpeters.com

10 9 8 7 6 5 4 3 2 1

Text © David T. Smith & Keli Rivers 2024.
Design and photographs
© Ryland Peters & Small 2024.

ISBN: 978-1-78879-588-3

A CIP record for this book is available
from the British Library.
US Library of Congress CIP data
has been applied for.

Printed in China

Author dedications:
*To EZ and to VK, who finally
got to Tommy's.*

*To Tamir, Jessica, Keith,
Rafa, Topher and Nicholas
who know the 'delights' of
juicing that extra case of
limes for service.*

Contents

Introduction

IN ITS JUST OVER ONE HUNDRED YEARS OF HISTORY, THE
MARGARITA HAS BECOME ONE OF THE MOST SUCCESSFUL
COCKTAILS OF ALL TIME. IT IS OFTEN RANKED IN THE TOP
THREE FAVOURITE COCKTAILS WORLDWIDE AND HAS
INSPIRED RESTAURANTS, SONGS, MERCHANDISE AND
OTHER TECHNOLOGICAL PARAPHERNALIA – SOME OF
WHICH CAN EVEN BE FOUND IN THE SMITHSONIAN.

The Margarita also has the other typical traits of a cocktail phenomenon: well-known variations (e.g. Frozen, Strawberry and Tommy's); a lively debate about garnishes; and options on how best to serve it, whether on-the-rocks, straight-up (without ice) or the dirty dump (where the ice used for shaking is poured along with the drink into the glass).

Margarita means 'daisy' in Spanish, and it is a member of the daisy family of drinks. Early published Margarita recipes were actually labelled as the Tequila Daisy. A daisy is a drink consisting of spirit and citrus that is balanced by a sweetener and includes the addition of a sweet liqueur to provide flavour and texture. Other examples include the Sidecar and the Cosmopolitan. Without the liqueur, the drink would be classed as a sour, belonging to the same drink family as the Gimlet and the Daiquiri.

Today, the Margarita has helped to propel the once unknown agave spirit of Tequila to its place as one of the 21st century's rising spirit stars.

The Margarita is a personal drink to many, and different people have their own idea of the perfect recipe. Some may have a preferred glass or brand of tequila, whilst others may add a family secret ingredient; such as a splash of kirschwasser.

Despite comprising only three ingredients, there is plenty of scope for creativity. When it comes to citrus, lemon is probably the most common juice substituted for lime, and this creates a more acidic and sour Margarita. White grapefruit juice, on the other hand, adds a distinct, crisp bitterness (one for the Negroni fan) and pink grapefruit juice makes a significantly sweeter drink, but with more acidity. For those who like a Paloma cocktail, substituting ruby grapefruit juice adds a lovely softness and slightly chocolatey notes.

Although this book, at times, calls for specific brands of tequila or mezcal, these are just a guide; the recipes have been designed to be enjoyed with whatever you have available. These recipes, along with your imagination, will hopefully help you find your way to your own marvellous Margarita moments.

TO RIM THE GLASS

Take a plate where the well (the dip) is slightly larger than the diameter of your glass and add your seasoning to the plate. Dampen the rim of the glass with a quartered lemon or lime – be generous, as this is what will make the seasoning stick to the glass – and gently rotate the rim on the plate to pick up the seasoning evenly.

Salt is the most common seasoning used in this way. Coarse salt or salt flakes stick to the glass better than finer table salt and also tend to have a bolder flavour.

Flavoured salts are commercially available, but these can quickly lose their potency once opened, so the best are always made freshly on the day.

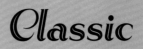

Classic Margarita

THE ORIGINAL 'TEQUILA DAISY' IS A SIMPLE YET SATISFYING
MIX OF TEQUILA, LIME AND ORANGE LIQUEUR.

50 ml/1¾ oz. agave spirit of choice
(such as blanco tequila)

20 ml/¾ oz. orange liqueur (such as Cointreau)

15 ml/½ oz. freshly squeezed lime juice

salt and lime wheel or wedge, to garnish

Serves 1

Shake the ingredients vigorously with ice.

Some recipes call for the addition of sugar (simple) syrup; this comes from a time when the tart Key lime was the main variety available in the USA. Today, the sweeter Persian lime – a hybrid between a Key lime and a lemon – is dominant, so the extra sugar is usually unnecessary. If you do use Key limes, you might want to add 5–10 ml/ 1–2 teaspoons sugar syrup.

TO SERVE

Straight-up: fine-strain the drink into a salt-rimmed, chilled cocktail glass and garnish with a wheel of lime.

On-the-rocks: empty the entire contents of the shaker, including the ice, into a salt-rimmed rocks glass (this is known as a 'dirty dump'). Top up with extra ice, if desired, and garnish with a lime wedge.

Picador

ONE OF THE EARLIEST RECORDED RECIPES THAT IS REASONABLY RECOGNISABLE AS A MODERN MARGARITA IS THE PICADOR FROM THE 1937 CAFÉ ROYAL COCKTAIL BOOK, BY WILLIAM J. CARLING.

50 ml/1¾ oz. blanco tequila (such as Ocho Blanco)

25 ml/¾ oz. Cointreau

25 ml/¾ oz. freshly squeezed lime juice

Serves 1

Shake the ingredients vigorously with ice and fine-strain into a cocktail glass.

TOREADOR
Also from the 1937 Café Royal Cocktail Book, the Toreador is made as above, but replace the Cointreau with apricot brandy liqueur.

MATADOR
Add 60 ml/2 oz. pineapple juice and serve in a tall, ice-filled glass.

ESPADOR
Replace the Cointreau with sloe gin, and the lime juice with lemon juice.

Tommy's Margarita

THIS IS PERHAPS THE MOST FAMOUS VARIATION ON THE MARGARITA. IT HAS ONE SMALL – BUT IMPORTANT – CHANGE: THE ORANGE LIQUEUR IS REPLACED BY AGAVE SYRUP, WHICH PROVIDES THE SWEETNESS NEEDED TO BALANCE OUT THE TARTNESS OF THE LIME. IT WAS INVENTED AFTER JULIO BERMEJO STARTED BARTENDING AT HIS PARENTS' (ELMY & TOMMY'S) MEXICAN RESTAURANT IN SAN FRANCISCO IN 1987.

50 ml/1¾ oz. blanco tequila
(such as Hornitos Blanco)

20 ml/¾ oz. freshly squeezed lime juice

10 ml/¼ oz. agave syrup

salt or sugar and lime wheel, to garnish

Serves 1

Shake all the ingredients vigorously with ice. Fine-strain into a salt- or sugar-rimmed cocktail glass and garnish with a wheel of lime.

BUZZ'S MARGARITA

Replace the agave spirit with honey, which provides rich, floral flavours.

MAPLE'S MARGARITA

Replace the agave syrup with maple syrup for a smooth 'like buttah' texture and a hint of nutty woodiness.

Frozen Margarita

THE ORIGINS OF THE FROZEN OR BLENDED MARGARITA APPEAR TO GO BACK TO 1947, SOME TEN YEARS AFTER THE EARLIEST RECIPE FOR THE ORIGINAL.

60 ml/2 oz. agave spirit of choice (such as Sauza Blanco Tequila)

15 ml/½ oz. freshly squeezed lime juice

15 ml/½ oz. orange liqueur

6 roughly 2.5-cm/1-in. ice cubes

salt and lime wheel, to garnish

Serves 1

Combine all the ingredients for 30–40 seconds in a blender. Pour into a large classic margarita glass, garnished with a salt rim and wheel of lime. Store-bought or dispenser ice works particularly well, as the hole in the middle helps it blend more easily.

Whiskeyrita

CORN WHISKEY GIVES A COMPLEMENTARY SWEETNESS WITH A TOUCH OF TORTILLA CHIPS.

50 ml/1¾ oz. corn whiskey (such as Mellow Corn)

50 ml/1¾ oz. Simple Margarita Mix (see right)

6 roughly 2.5-cm/1-in. ice cubes

lime wedges and mint, to garnish

Serves 1

Blend the ingredients for 30 seconds. Pour into a rocks glass and garnish with lime wedges and a sprig of mint.

SIMPLE MARGARITA MIX

Add 100 ml/3¼ oz. fine-strained lime juice, 100 ml/3¼ oz. Cointreau and 25 ml/¾ oz. white sugar to an air-tight bottle and shake to dissolve the sugar. Keep for 2 weeks in the fridge.

To Use Shake to remove any sediment and mix one part margarita mix to one part tequila. Serve on the rocks, or blend with ice for a frozen margarita.

Margarita de Oro

WHILST STARTING WITH THE BASICS OF AGAVE, LIQUEUR AND CITRUS JUICE, IT IS POSSIBLE TO BRANCH OUT AND EXPERIMENT WITH USING DIFFERENT LIQUEURS AND JUICES TO PRODUCE MARGARITA VARIATIONS. ONE OF THE MOST SUCCESSFUL SUBSTITUTES IS ORANGE JUICE (FRESHLY SQUEEZED MAKES ALL THE DIFFERENCE), WHICH PROVIDES A MORE ROUNDED, FRUITY AND INVITING CHARACTER WITH A TOUCH OF CREAMINESS.

50 ml/1¾ oz. blanco tequila
(such as Olmeca Altos Plata)
15 ml/½ oz. freshly squeezed orange juice
15 ml/½ oz. Mandarine Napoleon
(or other orange liqueur)
orange quarter-wheel, to garnish

Serves 1

Shake the ingredients vigorously with ice and fine-strain into a coupe glass. Garnish with a quarter-wheel of orange.

Sound of Sotol

SOTOL IS NOT AS WELL-KNOWN AS TEQUILA OR MEZCAL, BUT IT ALSO LENDS ITSELF TO MARGARITA-TYPE DRINKS. IT IS NOT MADE FROM AGAVE, BUT ANOTHER SPECIES OF DESERT FLORA CALLED 'DESERT SPOON'. IT MUST BE MADE IN THE MEXICAN STATES OF CHIHUAHUA, COAHUILA OR DURANGO.

50 ml/1¾ oz. sotol
  (such as La Higuera)
25 ml/¾ oz. Vault Aperitivo
  de Agave
15 ml/½ oz. Cointreau
twist of lemon peel, to garnish

Stir the ingredients thoroughly with ice in a mixing glass and strain into a classic martini glass. Garnish with a twist of lemon peel.

Serves 1

Raicilla Margarita

RAICILLA IS ANOTHER REGIONAL MEXICAN SPIRIT THAT IS USED TO MAKE MARGARITA-STYLE COCKTAILS. IT MUST BE MADE FROM 100% AGAVE AND PRODUCED IN THE STATES OF JALISCO OR NAYARIT.

50 ml/1¾ oz. raicilla
  (such as La Venenosa)
15 ml/½ oz. passion fruit liqueur
  (such as Passoa)
10 ml/¼ oz. freshly squeezed
  lime juice
100–150 ml/3¼–5¼ oz. tonic
  water
lime wheel and rosemary sprig,
  to garnish

Add the ingredients to an ice-filled glass and top up with tonic. Garnish with a lime wheel and a sprig of fresh rosemary.

Serves 1

Gin Daisy

THE MARGARITA'S COMBINATION OF SPIRIT, LIQUEUR AND CITRUS JUICE
MAKES IT A MEMBER OF THE DAISY FAMILY OF DRINKS. THIS GIN DAISY
IS A BRIGHT AND CRISP DRINK THAT ALLOWS THE GIN TO SING.

60 ml/2 oz. Sipsmith London dry gin

15 ml/½ oz. Curaçao

15 ml/½ oz. freshly squeezed
   lemon juice

soda water, to taste

Serves 1

Shake the first three ingredients vigorously with ice and then fine-strain into a champagne coupe. Add a splash of soda water to taste.

Santa Cruz Daisy

FANS OF THE DAIQUIRI MAY SEE SOME RESEMBLANCE IN THIS RECIPE. IN
FACT, ADD 15 ML/½ OZ. OF GRAPEFRUIT JUICE AND YOU'LL ESSENTIALLY
HAVE A PAPA DOBLE (HEMINGWAY DAIQUIRI). THE RUM COMPLEMENTS
THE FLORAL AND FRUITY MARASCHINO AND TART CITRUS. GRAB YOUR
PANAMA AND LET'S HEAD FOR THE KEYS!

60 ml/2 oz. aged rum
   (such as Smith & Cross)

15 ml/½ oz. freshly squeezed
   lime juice

15 ml/½ oz. Maraschino

sparkling or soda water, to taste

lime wedge, to garnish

Serves 1

Shake the first three ingredients vigorously with ice. Pour over ice in a tumbler or rocks glass and top up with sparkling or soda water. Garnish with a lime wedge.

Contemporary

The Carajillo Martini

THIS MARGARITA, MADE WITH COFFEE, IS DESIGNED TO BE ENJOYED AS AN AFTER-DINNER TREAT. LICOR 43 IS A COMPLEX HERBAL LIQUEUR. IF YOU ARE UNABLE TO FIND IT, BENEDICTINE ALSO WORKS VERY WELL.

20 ml/¾ oz. blanco tequila
   (such as Patrón Silver)

30 ml/1 oz. Licor 43

60 ml/2 oz. espresso coffee

3 espresso beans and grated
   Parmesan, to garnish

Serves 1

Shake the ingredients vigorously with ice and fine-strain into a large coupe glass. Garnish with three espresso beans and a pinch of finely grated Parmesan.

The Vallance

ANOTHER POST-MEAL DRINK, BUT THIS ONE IS MORE OF A DIGESTIF THANKS TO THE INCLUSION OF THE HERBAL LIQUEUR, CHARTREUSE.

50 ml/1¾ oz. blanco tequila
   (such as Hussong's Silver)

15 ml/½ oz. ruby red grapefruit
   juice

20 ml/¾ oz. Green Chartreuse

twist of lemon peel, to garnish

Serves 1

Shake the ingredients thoroughly with ice and fine-strain into a small cocktail glass. Garnish with a twist of lemon peel.

Becky (Long Margarita)

IF MARGARITA MEANS 'DAISY' IN SPANISH, THEN A LONG (OR TALL) VERSION SHOULD SURELY BE NAMED AFTER THE TALLEST SPECIES OF DAISY, LEUCANTHEMUM (SHASTA DAISY), OFTEN MORE SIMPLY REFERRED TO AS 'BECKY'.

50 ml/1¾ oz. blanco tequila or mezcal (such as Ilegal Mezcal Joven)

20 ml/¾ oz. orange liqueur

15 ml/½ oz. freshly squeezed lime juice

100 ml/3¼ oz. sparkling, soda or seltzer water

lime wedge, to garnish

Serves 1

Add the first three ingredients to a tall glass and stir. Fill with ice and top-up with your choice of water. Garnish with a lime wedge.

Note: You may use a tall glass rimmed with Tajín (spicy lime salt), as pictured, if liked.

Batanga

ANOTHER LONG DRINK WITH A NOD TO THE MARGARITA. THE INTERACTION BETWEEN THE SMOKE OF THE AGAVE AND THE SWEET, SPICY COLA IS SIMPLY SUPERB. FOR AN EXTRA FRUITY COCKTAIL, TRY USING THE GERMAN SODA, MEZZO MIX, WHICH IS A MIXTURE OF COLA AND ORANGE SODA. .

50 ml/1¾ oz. blanco tequila or mezcal (such as Ilegal Mezcal Blanco)

15 ml/½ oz. freshly squeezed lime juice

100 ml/3¼ oz. cola

lime wheels, to garnish

Serves 1

Add the first two ingredients to a tall glass and stir. Fill with ice and top-up with cola. Garnish with wheels of lime.

Nudo

THIS COCKTAIL IS INSPIRED BY THE ITALIAN PALATE CLEANSER COCKTAIL SGROPPINO, WHICH MEANS 'TO UNTIE A LITTLE KNOT'; 'NUDO' IS 'KNOT' IN SPANISH AND THIS DRINK COMBINES BLANCO AGAVE SPIRIT, LIMONCELLO AND SORBET WITH A DASH OF LIME.

50 ml/1¾ oz. Agalia Italian Agave Spirit
  (blanco tequila also works)

20 ml/¾ oz. limoncello

10 ml/¼ oz. freshly squeezed lime juice

2 tablespoons lemon sorbet

prosecco, to taste

grated lime zest, to garnish

Serves 2

Shake the tequila, limoncello and lime juice with ice and fine-strain into two champagne coupes, splitting the mix evenly between them. Add a tablespoon of sorbet to each glass and top up with prosecco. Garnish with a light sprinkle of grated lime zest.

Chelada

A CHELADA (LIKE THE MICHELADA, BELOW) COMBINES THE MARGARITA WITH ANOTHER REFRESHING BEVERAGE – BEER. MEXICAN FAVOURITES, SUCH AS CORONA, SOL OR MODELO, ARE GREAT CHOICES, BUT ANY LAGER WILL WORK. UNUSUALLY, THESE DRINKS ARE BOTH SERVED OVER ICE.

30 ml/1 oz. blanco tequila
15 ml/½ oz. freshly squeezed lime juice
1 bottle lager beer
lime wedge, to garnish

Serves 1

Add the ingredients to a tall, ice-filled glass rimmed with Tajín (spicy lime salt). Garnish with a lime wedge.

MICHELADA
For a Michelada, combine 2 dashes of Worcestershire sauce, 2 dashes of Tabasco sauce, a pinch of cayenne pepper and a pinch of salt before adding the ingredients for a Chelada (see above). Once again, this is served over ice, but with a rim of Sal Limón (salt with citric acid). An alternative is to use a 50:50 mix of salt and powdered sherbet.

Fantasy Margarita

MANY OF THE ORANGE LIQUEURS INTEGRAL TO THE MARGARITA RECIPE ARE CLEAR OR ORANGE, BUT CURAÇAO IS ALSO AVAILABLE IN SHADES OF RED, GREEN AND, OF COURSE, BLUE. AN EYE-CATCHING DRINK MADE WITH ONE OF THESE WILL TAKE YOU ONE STEP CLOSER TO THE BEACH.

20 ml/¾ oz. blanco tequila
   (such as Rooster Rojo Blanco)

10 ml/¼ oz. mezcal

20 ml/¾ oz. freshly squeezed lemon juice

20 ml/¾ oz. blue curaçao

20 ml/¾ oz. Lillet Blanc

blue sherbet and a twist of lemon peel, to garnish

Serves 1

Shake the ingredients vigorously with ice. Fine-strain into a cocktail glass rimmed with blue sherbet and garnish with a twist of lemon peel.

Open Sesame

THIS UNIQUE COMBINATION BRINGS TOGETHER THE COOL CRISPNESS
OF CUCUMBER WITH THE SUBTLE AROMATIC NUTTINESS OF SESAME OIL.

8 thick slices of cucumber

2 pinches of salt

45 ml/1¾ oz. blanco tequila

20 ml/¾ oz. freshly squeezed lime juice

15 ml/½ oz. triple sec

¼ teaspoon sesame oil

soda water, to taste

salt and cucumber slice, to garnish

Serves 1

Muddle the cucumber with the salt in a shaker.
Add the other ingredients except for the soda
water and shake vigorously with ice. Fine-strain
into a salt-rimmed tall glass and top up with
soda water. Garnish with a long slice
of cucumber.

Strawberry Margarita

A CLASSIC MARGARITA WITH A FRUITY TWIST.

3–4 fresh strawberries, plus extra to garnish
50 ml/1¾ oz. blanco tequila (such as Don Fulano Blanco)
15 ml/½ oz. freshly squeezed lime juice
20 ml/¾ oz. Cointreau
strawberry sugar (see below) and mint, to garnish

Serves 1

Muddle the strawberries in the bottom of a cocktail shaker, add the other ingredients with ice, and shake vigorously. Fine-strain into a cocktail glass that is rimmed with strawberry sugar and garnish with a strawberry half and mint leaves. (To make strawberry sugar, mix one part crushed dried strawberries – we pick them out of a packet of muesli – with two parts sugar.)

FROZEN STRAWBERRY MARGARITA

Add the ingredients to a blender along with six medium ice cubes and blend for 30 seconds. This even works with frozen strawberries instead of ice!

WATERMELON MARGARITA

To make a watermelon version, substitute the strawberries for 3–4 chunks of watermelon flesh.

Experimental

Tex-Mex Marga-tini

THIS FLAVOURFUL DRINK GOES VERY WELL WITH MEXICAN-INSPIRED CUISINE.

60 ml/2 oz. tequila reposado/anejo
   (such as Sauzo Repo)

30 ml/1 oz. Cointreau

30 ml/1 oz. freshly squeezed
   lime juice

10 ml/¼ oz. olive brine (cold)

splash of orange juice

salt, olives and lime wedge,
   to garnish

Serves 1

Shake the ingredients vigorously with ice and fine-strain into a cocktail glass with a half-salted rim. Garnish with three olives and a lime wedge.

Lola's Taquorita

JUST LIKE THE TEX-MEX MARGA-TINI, THIS MEXICAN-INSPIRED DRINK IS PERFECT SERVED WITH A BOWL OF TORTILLA CHIPS.

50 ml/1¾ oz. tequila blanco
   (such as 100 Años Blanco)

15 ml/½ oz. freshly squeezed
   lime juice

10 ml/¼ oz. Cointreau

10 ml/¼ oz. corn liqueur

10 ml/¼ oz. Ancho Reyes verde chilli
   liqueur

Serves 1

Shake all the ingredients vigorously with ice, and then fine-strain into a cocktail glass.

Chocolate-lime Margarita

A DELICIOUS DESSERT COCKTAIL COMBINING THE ZING OF THE MARGARITA AND THE INDULGENCE OF ANOTHER MEXICAN FAVOURITE, CHOCOLATE.

50 ml/1¾ oz. blanco tequila

15 ml/½ oz. freshly squeezed lime juice

10 ml/¼ oz. Cointreau

10 ml/¼ oz. crème de cacao (chocolate liqueur; my favourite is Tempus Fugit's Crème de Cacao)

chocolate shavings, to garnish

Serves 1

Shake the ingredients vigorously with ice and fine-strain into a stemmed glass with a rim of chocolate shavings.

CHOCOLATE-MINT MARGARITA
Replace the Cointreau with crème de menthe to create a Chocolate-Mint Margarita.

CHOCOLATE-ORANGE MARGARITA
By replacing the lime juice with freshly squeezed orange juice, you can make yourself a Chocolate-Orange Margarita.

Margaroni

A HYBRID WITH ANOTHER POPULAR SUMMER COCKTAIL, THE NEGRONI. THE WOOD NOTES OF THE REPOSADO WORK WELL WITH THE BITTER-SWEETNESS OF THE LIQUEUR, WHILST THE ORANGE JUICE ADDS A SUCCULENT SWEETNESS.

50 ml/1¾ oz. reposado tequila (such as Don Fulano)

30 ml/1 oz. Campari (if using Aperol instead, use 20 ml/¾ oz.)

20 ml/¾ oz. freshly squeezed orange juice (if using Aperol, use 30 ml/1 oz.)

20 ml/¾ oz. freshly squeezed lime juice

pink salt and lemon and lime moons, to garnish

Serves 1

Shake the ingredients vigorously with ice and fine-strain into an ice-filled glass half-rimmed with salt (ideally pink salt for added visual effect) and garnish with moons (half-circle slices) of lemon and lime.

The woodiness of the tequila gives this drink a slightly spicy, grassy depth that you don't get in the gin variation, whilst the combination of fruit juices provides a succulent, summery boost.

You can substitute the Campari for Aperol and adjust the recipe as noted above. This is especially good if you are using a blanco tequila or mezcal.

Tabasco Rascal

A FUN DRINK THAT WORKS WELL AS A DESSERT COCKTAIL, BUT WITH A GENTLE SURPRISE FROM THE TABASCO. NOT TO BE UNDERESTIMATED BY ITS APPEARANCE. THE DRINK IS RICH AND SUCCULENT AND EXTREMELY SIPPABLE. THE PASSION FRUIT LIQUEUR ADDS A TOUCH OF SUN-KISSED SHORES, WHILST THE MARMALADE COMPLEMENTS THE CURAÇAO. THE TABASCO ADDS A PLAYFUL NOTE THAT BALANCES OUT THE SWEET FRUITINESS OF THE DRINK, ADDING ONLY A MILD HEAT.

50 ml/1¾ oz. blanco tequila

30 ml/1 oz. Golden Moon Curaçao
(or other orange liqueur)

30 ml/1 oz. freshly squeezed lime juice

15 ml/½ oz. passion fruit liqueur (such as Passoa)

1 tablespoon (or one mini pot) orange marmalade

3–4 dashes Tabasco (if you like mild spice)
or 5–6 dashes (medium spice)

sprinkles or sugar strands, to garnish

Serves 1

Shake the ingredients vigorously with ice and fine-strain into a large cocktail glass with a rim of sprinkles or sugar strands.

Concorde Margarita

A COCKTAIL INSPIRED BY THE SHORT-LIVED CONCORDE AIR SERVICE BETWEEN
PARIS AND MEXICO CITY BETWEEN 1978 AND 1982, THIS DRINK EMBRACES
SOME OF THE BEST SPIRITS THAT BOTH OF THESE COUNTRIES HAVE TO
OFFER. THE RICH, DECADENT AND OH-SO 80S WOODY NOTES OF THE SPIRITS
COMPLEMENT THE INDULGENT ORANGE NOTES OF THE GRAND MARNIER.
THE SUGAR RIM ADDS BALANCE TO THIS LIGHTLY TART DRINK. FOR A LONGER
VARIATION, TOP-UP THE GLASS WITH SODA WATER OR DRY GINGER ALE.

25 ml/¾ oz. reposado tequila
(such as Olmeca Altos Reposado)

25 ml/¾ oz. Cognac (such as Courvoisier VS or VSOP)

25 ml/¾ oz. Grand Marnier

25 ml/¾ oz. freshly squeezed lemon juice

brown sugar and twist of orange peel, to garnish

Serves 1

Shake the ingredients vigorously with ice.
Fine-strain into an ice-filled and brown-sugar-
rimmed brandy balloon (the larger the better!)
and garnish with orange peel.

The Working Girl

INDULGE IN THIS DELIGHTFUL BLEND OF TEQUILA, FRAGRANT ORANGE BLOSSOM AND CREAMY ORGEAT, WHICH CREATES A RICH AND LUXURIOUS TEXTURE. WITH EACH SIP, YOU'LL BE TRANSPORTED TO SUN-KISSED BEACHES AND VIBRANT CITRUS GROVES.

50 ml/1¾ oz. tequila reposado

20 ml/¾ oz. orgeat (almond) syrup

30 ml/1 oz. freshly squeezed lemon juice

3 dashes orange blossom water

soda water, to taste

grated nutmeg, to garnish

Serves 1

Shake all the ingredients except for the soda water vigorously with ice and fine-strain into a large coupe glass. Top up with soda water and garnish with a sprinkle of grated nutmeg.

Seasonal

Candy Cane Margarita

A FESTIVE MARGARITA THAT CERTAINLY LOOKS THE PART, WITH VIBRANT GREEN NEATLY CONTRASTING WITH THE RED CHERRY GARNISH. THE DRINK HAS A LIGHT MENTHOL NOTE, SIMILAR TO THE POPULAR CHRISTMAS CANDY.

50 ml/1¾ oz. blanco tequila

25 ml/¾ oz. freshly squeezed lime juice

15 ml/½ oz. Cointreau

10 ml/¼ oz. green crème de menthe

candy cane and cherry, to garnish

Serves 1

Shake the ingredients vigorously with ice and fine-strain into a chilled, stemmed glass. Garnish with a mini candy cane and a red cherry.

Merry Margarita

THIS CHRISTMASSY COCKTAIL IS LOVELY SERVED WITH A SQUARE OF CHRISTMAS CAKE ON THE SIDE.

60 ml/2 oz. blanco tequila

15 ml/½ oz. freshly squeezed lime juice

15 ml/½ oz. sweet cream sherry

2–3 dashes angostura bitters

twist of orange peel, to garnish

Serves 1

Shake the ingredients vigorously with ice and fine-strain into a cocktail glass. Garnish with a twist of orange peel.

Fresca Fiesta

THIS DRINK TAKES AGUA FRESCA (MEANING FRESH OR COOL WATER) AS A BASE AND ADDS SOME MARGARITA MAGIC.

50 ml/1¾ oz. blanco tequila (for a heartier drink use blanco mezcal, and for a fruitier, smokier one use sotol)

20 ml/¾ oz. yuzu liqueur (such as Pierre Ferrand Dry Curaçao Yuzu)

100 ml/3¼ oz. homemade agua fresca (see below)

mint, to garnish

Serves 2

Add the ingredients to an ice-filled glass and stir. Garnish with a sprig of mint.

The Japanese yuzu adds a lovely lemon-lime floral note, but if you can't find a yuzu liqueur, don't worry, an orange liqueur will also work.

HOMEMADE AGUA FRESCA

750 ml/25 oz. still water (cold)

2–3 hibiscus tea bags

25 ml/¾ oz. freshly squeezed lime juice

25 ml/¾ oz. granulated white sugar

Allow the hibiscus tea bags and cold water to combine in a large jug/pitcher for an hour. Remove the tea bags and add the lime juice and sugar. Stir until the sugar has dissolved and then add ice to serve.

Piñas Locas

A RATHER EXTRAVAGANT SERVE, BUT ONE THAT WILL MAKE YOU THE ENVY OF ANY OTHER DRINKERS AROUND YOU! A FRUITY AND SUCCULENT DRINK THAT PROVIDES EXCELLENT SUMMER REFRESHMENT.

50 ml/1¾ oz. blanco tequila
(or 50/50 tequila and mezcal)
30 ml/1 oz. fresh pineapple juice
20 ml/¾ oz. freshly squeezed lime juice
8 ml/1½ teaspoons agave syrup
Tajín seasoning and coriander/cilantro, to garnish

Serves 1

Shake the ingredients vigorously with ice and fine-strain into an ice-filled, hollowed-out pineapple (or other suitable large glass). Sprinkle the rim of the pineapple with Tajín seasoning and garnish with a sprig of fresh coriander/cilantro.

St. Martin's Sunrise

AN AUTUMNAL/FALL MARGARITA THAT IS PART-MARGARITA, PART-TEQUILA SUNRISE. THE MASALA SALT RIM ADDS A TOUCH OF COMPLEX SPICE, WHILST THE MEZCAL PROVIDES A TOUCH OF BONFIRE-LIKE SMOKE. A REFRESHING, YET COSY DRINK TO ENJOY AS THE SUMMER SLOWLY FADES AWAY.

50 ml/1¾ oz. blanco tequila

10 ml/¼ oz. mezcal (optional, for a little extra smoke)

20 ml/¾ oz. freshly squeezed lime juice

50 ml/1¾ oz. freshly squeezed orange juice

5–10 ml/1–2 teaspoons grenadine

masala spice and salt (see below) and orange peel, to garnish

Serves 1

Shake the ingredients vigorously with ice and fine-strain into a tall, ice-filled glass with a masala spice and salt rim. Add the grenadine by slowly pouring it down the inside of the glass. Garnish with orange peel.

For the deliciously savoury masala spice and salt rim, combine 1 part masala spice mix to 3 parts salt.

May the 4th Margarita

TO CELEBRATE A GALAXY FAR, FAR AWAY, WILL YOU OPT FOR THE
LIGHT OR THE DARK SIDE? OR MAYBE TRY A LITTLE BIT OF BOTH?

LIGHT SIDE

50 ml/1¾ oz. blanco tequila

20 ml/¾ oz. Dolin Blanc Vermouth

30 ml/1 oz. grapefruit juice

30 ml/1 oz. soda water

white salt and a lime wheel, to garnish

DARK SIDE

50 ml/1¾ oz. anejo tequila

20 ml/¾ oz. Amaro Montenegro
  (alternatively, use an intense red vermouth)

30 ml/1 oz. grapefruit juice

8 ml/1½ teaspoons agave syrup

30 ml/1 oz. soda water

black lava sea salt and grapefruit wedge,
  to garnish

Serves 1

Shake the ingredients except for the
soda water vigorously with ice.

Pour into a salt-rimmed ice-filled rocks
glass (use white salt for the Light Side and
Hawaiian black lava sea salt for the Dark Side
– don't get the Himalayan variety as it stinks
of sulphur!), top-up with soda water and
garnish with lime or grapefruit.

Hot-buttered Margarita

THE BUTTER ADDS A LOVELY CREAMINESS TO THIS DRINK, COMPLEMENTED BY THE SWEETNESS OF THE LIQUEUR AND SYRUP AND THE SHARPNESS OF THE LIME JUICE.

20 ml/¾ oz. reposado tequila

10 ml/¼ oz. freshly squeezed lime juice

10 ml/¼ oz. Grand Marnier

5–10 ml/1–2 teaspoons sugar syrup

60 ml/2 oz. boiling water

1 heaped teaspoon lightly salted butter

Serves 1

Stir the first four ingredients (not the boiling water or butter) without ice and then pour into a heat-proof glass. Top up with boiling water, add the butter, and gently stir.

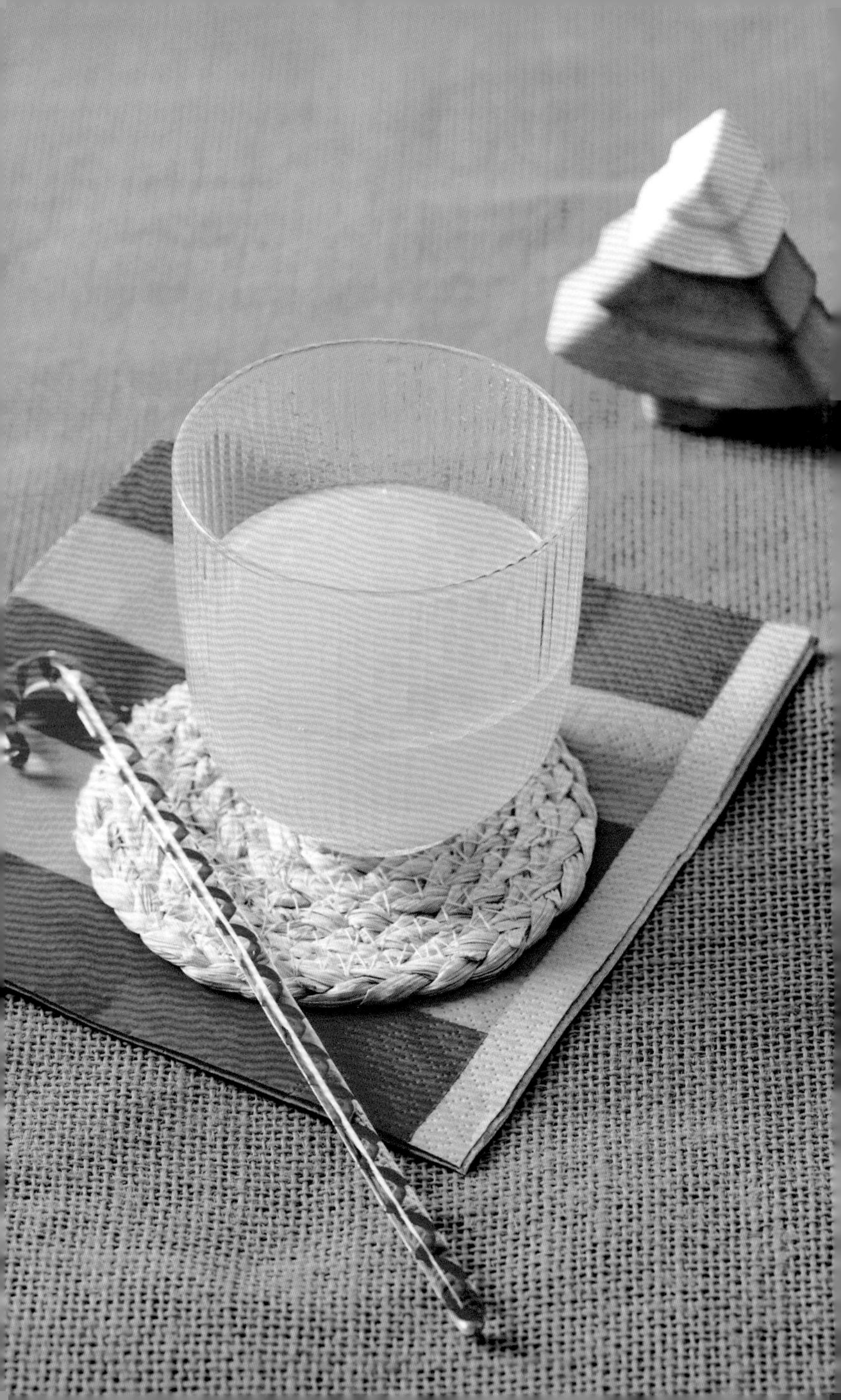

One Minute to Margarita

FOR A GAUDY GARNISH, TAPE A SMALL COCKTAIL SPARKLER TO THE SIDE OF THE GLASS AND LIGHT. BE SURE TO REMOVE AND DISPOSE OF THE SPARKLER CAREFULLY ONCE IT HAS GONE OUT AND BEFORE DRINKING, OR YOU MIGHT END UP WITH A SINGED EYEBROW OR WORSE!

50 ml/1¾ oz. blanco tequila

25 ml/¾ oz. freshly squeezed lime juice

25 ml/¾ oz. Cointreau Noir

15 ml/½ oz. Champagne

Serves 1

Add all of the ingredients except the Champagne to a shaker with ice. Shake vigorously and fine-strain into a cocktail glass. Top-up with Champagne.

Index

Acknowledgements

Sara L. Smith without whom none of our books would be possible, The Zandonas, Queenie & Big T, J.P. Smith, DWS, Hazza Smith, Dot & Pete, JP Barber & Becky, The Gin Genies, The Bear & Cubs, The Gin Archive, The Martini Police, AK Katy & Juan, Stupot, Lorro, Lolly, Julesy, DAB Gin & Dan Miller, VP (la dolce Bella) Piromallo, Jon, Gin Queen, Jaye, Rosie t' Bear & Harry limes, Big Bad Bernie & Dr. Damo, SJ Rex, TobTobs, DingDing, Shannon Tebay, Bazza M, Nita A, Little Nelly, Alex and Speciality Drinks, The Owens, The Haymans, Haley Perry, Ridders, Joel, Alice Lascelles, Jimmy B, Lexi Turner, Hannah BTW, Paola, Spirits Business, Paragraph, Chockie, Zaloren, Steph DC, IWSC, C-Dog, Jussi, Eric BarCart, Maritza & Ben, Simone, (The Other) Dave Smith, Ben (with the watch), Anne Jones, Paloma, Terrorvision, Oli and Emile, GinMonkey, D'Eagles, Paul Clarke, Camper, SG1.

Michelle & Jim Rivers, Sally & Andrew, Josh "Muddy" Rivers, Diamond Ken and his Sister Wives, Foxzilla, Zahra, Carla Verenzuela, Luis Navarro, Tyler Wang, Flashdance Nance & Jason, Allie "The Big Cheese" Klug, Kellie & Finn, BB, Sassy Chasse, Simon Brooking, Mo, Conner, Rich, Gardner, Davey Jones, Jonathan Armstrong, Edwin, Kay Quigley, Bobby G, Ugo, Michael Fawthrop, Adam Harris, Jesse Maguire, Kate McKiernan, The Donkeys, Janice Snowden, Dawn, Janice Bailon, The Gin Girl, Benjie Lawless Watterson, Zaltfunction, Josh and the Down & Out team, The Hotsy Totsy, the Fonda Team, Trad Room, Travel Bar, Chez Oskar, Bandits, Cotê Underground, Hawksmoor NYC, Crown Shy, Happy Accidents, Best Intentions, Tin Widow and every airport bartender working the early and late shifts! And last, but not least, Julia and her team at RPS.